Emma Johnson-Rivard's

THE WITCH'S CAT
AND HER FATEFUL MURDER BALLADS

The Esthetic Apostle

First published in the United States of America
by The Esthetic Apostle, 2018
Chicago, IL

Copyright © Emma Johnson-Rivard
All rights reserved

ISBN: 9781729497845

Cover Art by
Emma Johnson-Rivard

Interior Art Courtesy of
Martine Mooijenkind's
Spell Series

Acknowledgments

Dime Store Murder Story and *Legendary Wolves: In Memory of Peter Stumpp's Daughter* previous appeared in New Thoreau Quarterly. *Sister* previously appeared in Nixes Mate Review. *The Bear Cave, The Fish* and *I Discuss Suicide,* and *Androcles and the Lion, A Eulogy* previously appeared in The Write Launch. *A Babydyke's Primer to Slasher Films* and *The Language of the Outsider* previously appeared in Brickplight. *An Atheist In Trump's Americana* previously appeared in the Ocotillo Review. *Legendary Wolves: In Memory of Peter Stumpp's Daughter (Redux)* is set to appear in the Brooklyn Review. *Familiar* appeared in Meow Meow Pow Pow Lit. *wrecker* is set to appear in great weather for MEDIA. *Burial Ground* appeared in Typehouse Literary Magazine. *Scapegoat* is forthcoming in the Blood Puddles anthology. *The Painter Seeks A Muse* And *The Historian Lectures on Jack The Ripper* appeared in New Plains Review. *Drafting* has appeared in the Esthetic Apostle.

Contents

Familiar	6
Dime Store Murder Story	7
Fish Bride	8
Anatomy	9
To The Tragic Hero of Her Favorite Murder Ballad	10
Drafting	11
Muse	12
Bad Bitch Ode	13
Scapegoat	15
Androcles And The Lion, A Eulogy	18
Mercy	19
The Language Of The Outsider	20
The Painter Seeks A Muse And The Historian Lectures on Jack The Ripper	21
Pack Mentality	32
An Atheist In Trump's Americana	33
Legendary Wolves: In Memory of Peter Stumpp's Daughter	35
Burn Notice	36
scene: filmmaker seeks poet's advice on composition of sext to future wife	37
Various Thematic Punishments In The SAW Series	38
Halloween Prayer	39
Artemisia Gentileschi, Self Portrait As The Allegory of Painting (1639)	40
A Babydyke's Primer to Slasher Films	41
Georgia O'Keefe	42
Burial Ground	43
mice inherit apocalypse	44
Legendary Wolves: In Memory of Peter Stumpp's Daughter (Redux)	45
Ouroboros	53
Relic	54
wrecker	56

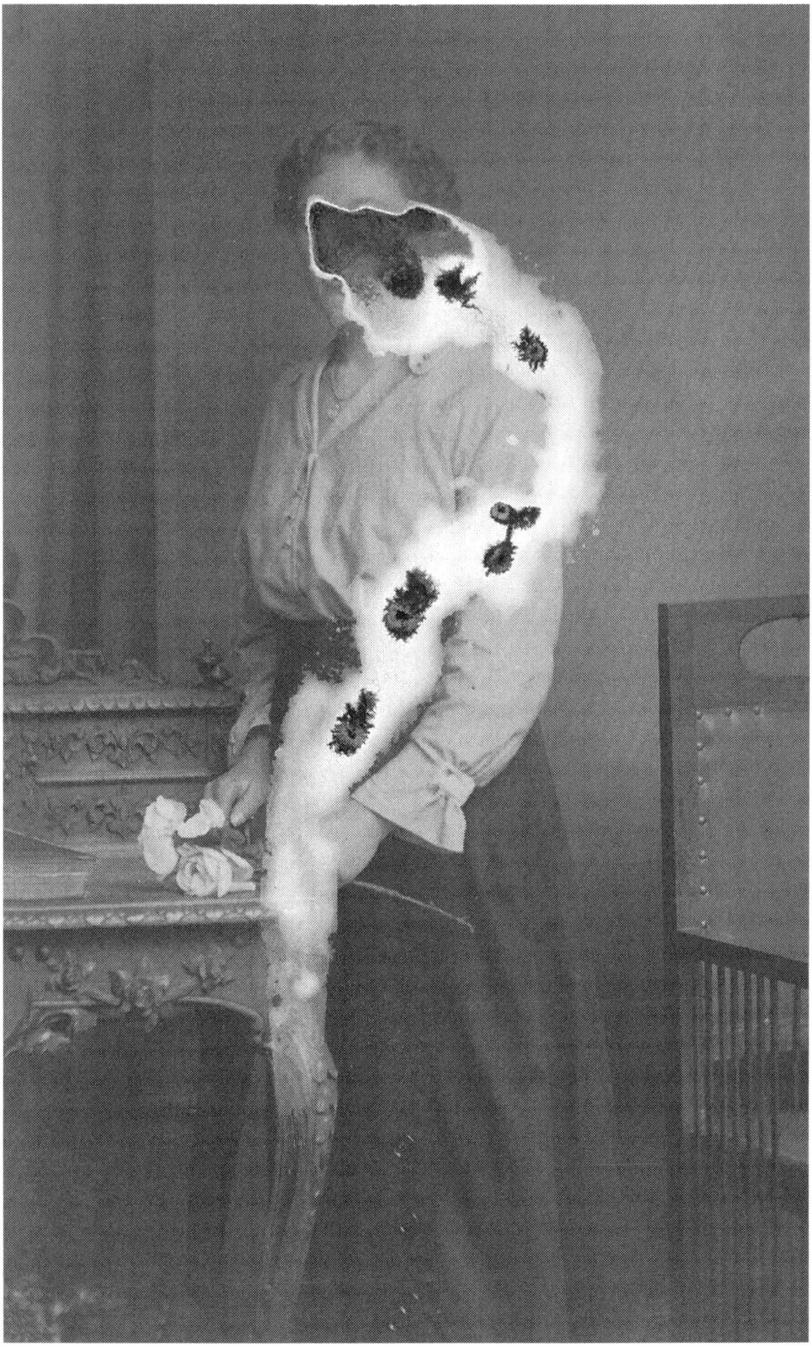

History does strange things to dead women.
Kelly Faircloth

Familiar

My cat was born small, had
too many claws, it was
no good for the soul.

Eternal, I dream of witches.
Kitten, do you know how they died?

It took ropes, stone. Men with laws.
I think about this often.

In Salem, all your witches
were strangers and
strange women.
Their cats lived, cried,
forever dreamt of fire.

Kitten to cat you will
remember me.

Dime Store Murder Story

The comfort of yarns;
it happens on a page, poetically
to someone else

Victim #5 in the library
with the revolver, then
Blame the butler

Rejoice in our conclusion
It is their wit that saves the day

Opening scene
        a woman named for a river
        dies by one, becomes
        the eternal victim

Tomorrow
        museums build shrines, worship
        at the ripper's knives

Return to Christie, Doyle
Track the killer, clever reader
Rejoice in your conclusion
and ink-bound justice done

Fish Bride

dead girl dawning she
drowned in the end, ending strong.
holy ghost for a holy song we sing
go down deep and dig up the bones.
sailor born with her fishbone brine
swallow. sorrow.
she dropped in a storm
strung a harp from her span of ribs, then
born again as a sunfish for you we
       sing

Anatomy

Formaldehyde in a wine glass, *hell
have you seen her dress?*

In high school, she dissected a pig
long dead, watched
a senior boy crush the skull
under his thumb.

Remember when they tore her dress?

I heard about the needles of her spine,
unbroken. The dress
was violet. She gave up
the ribbon of her corsage,
tied it sweet to my throat.

Hell. I remember.

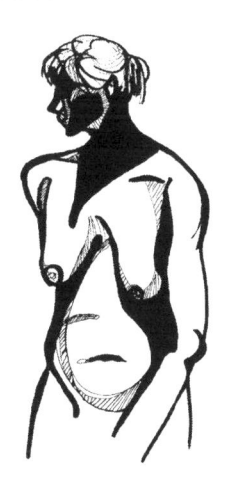

To the Tragic Hero of Her Favorite Murder Ballad

I care not for the flowers you left in her teeth.
You murdered a woman.
Your sorrow is nothing.

Drafting (After Kelly Hansen Maher)

at the start
i found my friend
hands wide and wet
with paint
and we laughed
before
asking how
it should change

at the start
i found my love
hands wide and wet
with sea foam
and we lived
before
asking why
it should end

Muse

to be a girl artist you must first
worship a girl artist.
she will be mad or dead, or
mad and dead, and you will wonder
where you fit, then
why wine makes you sick
and what her lover thought
if your girl artist of the morning
had a lover
and you will take that mourning,
mad girl, blood clot in the brain
give words to sorrow on
sunday and then
sunder, small thing:
put this in your heart.

Bad Bitch Ode

Wanna know something strange? Mary Shelley lost her virginity on her mother's grave. She kept her husband's stone heart in the big desk she wrote on. It wasn't the desk she wrote *Frankenstein* on, but I'm sure it was a beautiful piece of furniture nonetheless.

Mary Shelley was fucking metal.

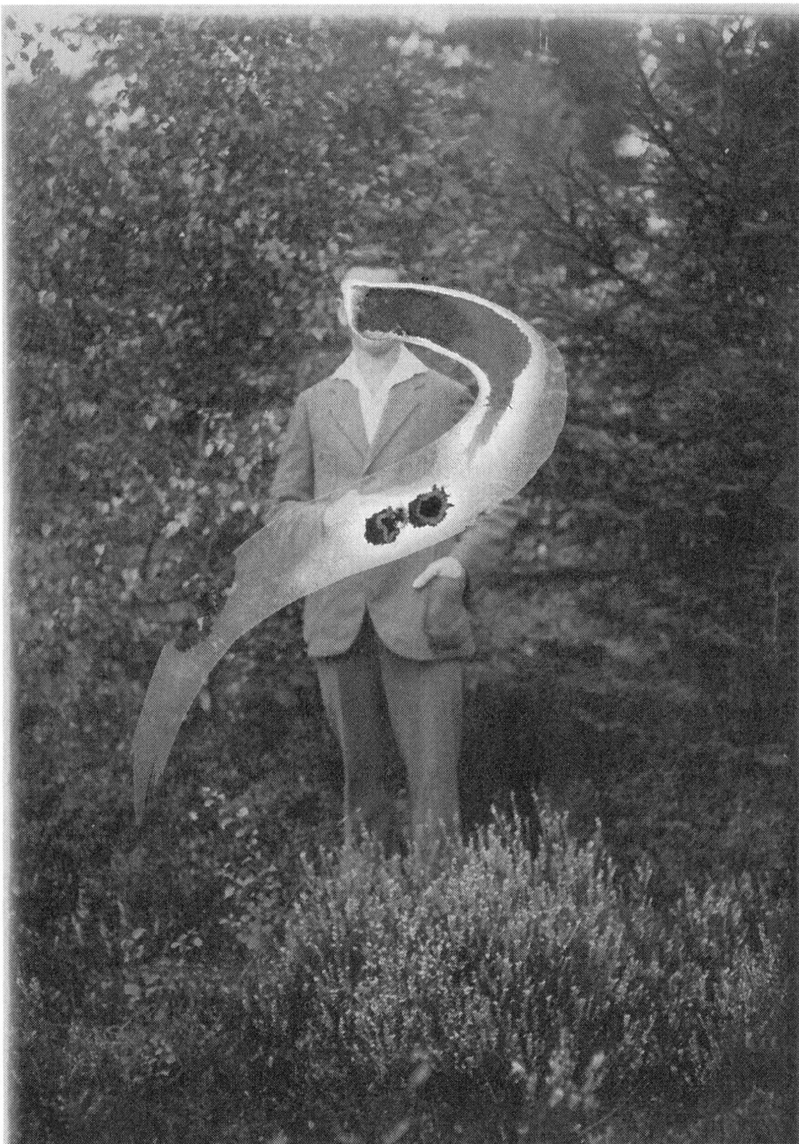

Scapegoat

Come down to the river and you'll find the girl there, the one sitting on the bank. She'll smile as she feeds sticks to the fire, smile as the smoke curls up through her hair. Come down to the river and you'll find a strange time. The girl, she snaps a stick in half, feeds the end to the fire, and motions you close.

She says, "I'm going to tell you a story."

She says, "Are you listening?"

Then: "Good. Because I'm gonna tell you about scapegoats. Used to be, folks thought they could get rid of all their bad shit - all the nasty stuff that goes through their heads that they really don't wanna do - if they took it out, you know, *symbolically*. So they'd go out away from the village, out into...whatever was out there. Let's say a desert. So they'd go into the desert with a big hammer and a bunch of nails, until they were really alone and maybe they were cold, but either way they were *gone* from the world. But they wouldn't be alone, exactly.

"Nah," says the girl. "They'd bring a goat with 'em. And once they were all good and gone, they'd let all their bad thoughts out and let 'em rip. Get them out in the air. But it was okay, 'cause it wasn't in the village, and nothing that happens in the desert - or the forest or the mountains or whatever they had back then - none of that stuff really *counts*, so long as it's out. So they'd take the hammer and the nails and they'd use all their darkness up on that goat and when they were done, they'd nail it to a rock and that was that. And it was good, 'cause then all their badness was stuck out there with the goat and not *inside*."

This is where she smiles. "Sucks to be the goat," she says. "Bet you're glad you're not a goat. But that's not the point and you're distracting me. Anyway, one time, this farmer had a son, and the son had some nastiness boiling up inside him. So the farmer says, '*Son, you ought to get out your hammer and your nails. I'll love you better when you're done.*'

"And if it'd been good times, the son would've done just that and everything would've been fine. But see, the farm had been going through some tough times, a famine of epic proportions, and all their goats were dead. So the son thought real hard about what he ought to do, because he couldn't just let that badness sit in his bones, oh no, it would get sour and eventually it would spill out and get its nastiness on everything. And - this part is important - the farmer said to his son, *'Everyone will love you better when you are undone, and your evil is nailed to goat bones out in the desert and not creeping through our halls. They cannot love you now. I cannot love you any longer while you are like this.'*"

Here the girl sighs. "And you know how people are, don't you? Even if you can't love anything, you want them to love *you*. So the son got to thinking. What would stand for a goat when all the goats were dead? So he went to the barn, but all their pigs had starved. So went to the fields but all their horses were gone. He even went to town looking for a bird, but they were all too fast and mean for him to catch. It was very late by the time the son came back to the farm, with his hammer and his nails and his hands still unbloodied, and no goat to show for it. His father was already asleep but the sister was there waiting for him at the gate. She said, *'Brother, why do you look so sad?'*

And he said to her, *'All the goats are dead.'*

'Well,' said the sister, *'you'll have to be clever then, won't you?'*

The son looked at her, and smiled then. (It's usually said that he was handsome). *'Yes, sister, I must be clever, mustn't I?'*

Well, morning came, and the farmer woke up to find his son gone. The farmer was pleased, thinking his son had gone out to purge his evil, and would surely be back soon and all would be well. So the farmer went about his business and in time the son came back to the gates carrying a hammer but no nails.

He smiled, with a bloody face, and said, '*Father, I am absolved. My evil is gone and you will love me all the more for it.*'

Indeed the farmer was very happy. '*Come, my dear child, come inside and your sister will fix us a meal in celebration. We have little but we have enough.*'

The son shook his head. '*Oh, father, my sister will not be coming.*'

'*Why not, my son?*' asked the farmer.

'*Father, my father, I needed her bones. My darkness needed out and we had no goats to give. She said I should be clever, father dear, and now I am returned. Are you not pleased?*'

Now the girl smiles. She feeds the fire again. "Be happy you're not a goat, friend."

Androcles And The Lion, A Eulogy

The problem with this fable is that I'm afraid of lions
and Androcles was still a slave when he left the ring

In some versions the lion eats him anyway
licks righteous blood from his paws and says
    It is but my nature, love
    I cannot be blamed

Even the voice that killed Abraham's reason wouldn't
judge a lion
and I am the eternal atheist in this story
however it is told

This is my truth, love.
Save the lion
ease his pain
and he'll grant you comfort
when the empires throw you to the ring

In the dust you will not die alone
The lion lays his bleeding paw upon your brow
and in this you are not baptized but remembered
The lion says
    I will kill them in your name, small
                                        thing
And that is my fable

For your kindness you are avenged
eternally

My love, they do not win

Mercy

My mother stole a cat once.
The neighbor wouldn't feed him, left him crying
in the bush, roses
for a collar.

He had knobby bones, a
mountain range of a spine
endless, hungry.

My mother said,
don't worry.
I did this for your heart.

The Language Of The Outsider

Part one: identification
knowing Other, then
yourself

The shapes used to track
go both ways

Next: understand
there are two ways to suffer
pain from hunger or
pain from truth

The poet is not a martyr if she starves
or a hero if she bleeds

Third: martyrs die. Who knows what they think?

Forth: the poet choses more than words.

Finally: the body is temporary.
The world in flux
but the word, oh

The word is eternal.

The Painter Seeks A Muse And The Historian Lectures on Jack The Ripper

A Short Play

CHARACTERS

The Historian　　　a young woman in college

The Painter　　　　a young woman in college

*Two friends sit drinking coffee.
The HISTORIAN carries a book bag.
The PAINTER has a portfolio and
is taking notes on a piece of paper.*

PAINTER

Be as honest as you can.

HISTORIAN

I wasn't aware people interviewed their muses.

PAINTER

I don't have to take notes, if that makes it easier.

HISTORIAN

Studies show that handwritten notes improve memory retention and increased comprehension of abstract concepts.

PAINTER

So...

HISTORIAN

Go ahead.

PAINTER

Thank you. I just wanted to say, you don't have to answer everything. I'd like you to be honest, but if there's anywhere you don't want me to go, just say so.

HISTORIAN

That's very polite of you.

PAINTER

I don't want to hurt anyone with my work unless I mean to.

HISTORIAN

Do you mean to hurt people?

PAINTER

Sometimes I mean to insult them or force you to see a painful truth. I mean "you" as the collective, not you personally, of course. I very rarely direct my work at specific, individual people, and only then to historical figures or politicians.

HISTORIAN

Because they expect it?

PAINTER

I suppose they do. But it's more because they've shifted into the background of our collective unconsciousness. They mean something more than themselves. And sometimes they cause great harm or great innovation by being more than themselves.

HISTORIAN

So a painting of Copernicus is more important than a painting of a crowd?

PAINTER

I wouldn't say it's more important. Just different. And I'd probably work with Galileo, anyway.

HISTORIAN

You're pretty good at this.

PAINTER

Thank you.

HISTORIAN

Do you write papers?

PAINTER

Sometimes. The collective you tends to think there's this great divide between painters and historians, but we're all academics, really. We take notes and draw conclusions.

HISTORIAN

And neither of us get rich.

The Painter laughs.

PAINTER

Nope! Though I'm supposed to be interviewing you.

HISTORIAN

My apologies. I got carried away.

PAINTER

That's fine. Do you mind if I begin?

HISTORIAN

Not at all.

PAINTER

Excellent. As I said, you don't have to answer if you don't want to. But I'd like you to be as honest as you can.

HISTORIAN

I understand.

PAINTER

Then I'll jump right in. Why do you study historical crime?

HISTORIAN

Why do I study it, or why should the collective you study it?

PAINTER

Both, please.

HISTORIAN

I research crimes concerning women; whether as perpetrators, bystanders, or victims. It became a fascination of mine in high school when I saw this movie about Jack the Ripper and I found myself wondering about the women. The ones who died, of course, but their families as well. Annie Chapman had three children. No one really talks about them.

PAINTER

She was the first victim?

HISTORIAN

Second. She was murdered on September 8th, 1880.

PAINTER

So you write about the Ripper.

HISTORIAN

No. I don't care about the Ripper.

PAINTER

Just the women.

HISTORIAN

Looking at the crimes is a way of looking at multiple levels of society all at once. How these women died is extremely well documented. Working backwards, I try to get a picture of how they lived.

PAINTER

Like with the Ripper.

HISTORIAN

I don't want to talk about him.

PAINTER

So why look at crimes at all? If you're interested in the lives of Victorian women,

PAINTER

I can think of other ways you could do it without encountering such gruesome history.

HISTORIAN

You're not the first person to ask me that. With this kind of history, it's easy to get drawn into the sensation of the narrative. Make a spectacle of the blood and guts. And I can't speak to why other people are drawn to this particular field, but for me, there was a profound sense of injustice that women like Annie Chapman are remembered for what was probably the worst moment of their lives. The reason people know her name is because she was murdered and the collective <u>we</u>, as you said, has developed this whole subculture around the person who killed her. You can buy replicas of the knife. People dress up as Gentleman Jack for Halloween. And the general consensus is that Annie and the others put themselves into dangerous situations and got <u>themselves</u> killed. The dominant narrative in this case is about the grand mystery of revealing the killer. It's treated as an intellectual puzzle and not a tragedy. The truth is, Annie Chapman and the other women died because a man who hated women decided to murder them because of it.

PAINTER

So you don't have any theories about who the Ripper was?

HISTORIAN

Everyone has theories. I have my own, but there's not enough evidence to prove them.

PAINTER

Does his identity matter at all?

HISTORIAN

I'm not saying we shouldn't look or that there's anything wrong with trying to figure it out. People have done very thoughtful, important work trying to close the case. It's too late for the victims and their families, but the pursuit of justice isn't something that should come with a time limit. But I also think that the whole conversation has shifted to putting this almost mythical killer on a pedestal.

                                                    HISTORIAN
It's become the legend of Jack the Ripper and his so called
"perfect murders" rather than a historical evil we should be
working to eradicate in the present. When we come to the
point where you've got people idealizing this kind of violence
against women, then you know we've got a problem.
                                                    PAINTER
What do you mean, idealizing the violence?
                                                    HISTORIAN
The Ripper has become a sort of folk hero, in the collective
consciousness. He's called a criminal genius, his crimes are
praised for how they were carried out. You can buy replicas
of the knife we think he used, for God's sake.
                                                    PAINTER
Is this something you find with a lot of the cases you study?
                                                    HISTORIAN
Occasionally, though never to this extreme as the Ripper case.
                                                    PAINTER
Why do you think that is?
                                                    HISTORIAN
Victorian crimes were reported to the public in a very
specific way. Information was released episodically and it
was purposefully sensationalized. Criminal cases and trials
were followed closely by the public. Executions were treated
like county fairs. People sold food, souvenirs; people made
a day out of it. The Ripper case also touched on a lot of
fears that people were grappling with at the time, but didn't
necessarily have an outlet to express. That time period in
London saw extreme wealth disparities, and tensions between
various ethnic and religious groups were quite high. People
were afraid. A lot of prejudice came out of the proverbial
woodwork because of it. And people in London, especially
around the Whitechapel area, lived in very close proximity to
each other, in horribly squalid conditions.

PAINTER
There wasn't any way to escape.

HISTORIAN
Exactly. The Ripper case brought a lot of that tension to the surface and so there was a great deal of interest in the case. But I'd say even back then, the crimes started developing a mythology of their own. "Jack can't be caught, he's a monster, a criminal mastermind", things like that. And of course he was never caught. The mystery appeals to people.

PAINTER
But there are a lot of unsolved crimes in the world.

HISTORIAN
Thousands. Part of the problem, at least from my perspective, is the facts of the case are consistently overshadowed by the legend. Jack the Ripper wasn't a criminal mastermind who just vanished into the night; the police didn't have access to what we would consider standard forensic tests, the victims were all vulnerable, and Whitechapel was a notoriously dark area. I mean that literally; there was a great deal of smog and the public street lamps of the time were quite weak. Furthermore, it wasn't difficult to avoid the police. We know from other accounts that the Whitechapel police wore a specific type of boot, and these boots made a distinct sound on the cobblestone roads. So even before a criminal would see a policeman, they would hear him coming. Add that to the fact that the patrol routes were predictable, and even a moderately clever criminal could avoid detection at night.

PAINTER
So Jack wasn't so special after all.

HISTORIAN
No. He was a criminal and he never saw justice for his crimes, but that was hardly unique for the time. People zero in on the legend rather than the facts of the case.

PAINTER
Given your feelings about the way the case is approached today, why research it at all?

HISTORIAN

I want to say because someone should do justice to the memory of the victims. And I do want that, I want these women to be seen as whole people instead of just props in the saga of Jack the Ripper, but I'm also very aware that I can't speak <u>for</u> these women. I can only speak <u>about</u> them. There's always a risk of turning them into props of my own; I'm not arrogant enough to think I'm above that.

PAINTER

That sounds difficult.

HISTORIAN

I believe we should be thoughtful about history, especially as it concerns violence against women. But just because something is difficult doesn't mean we shouldn't try.

PAINTER

I agree. If we never tried to engage with the past, how would we ever learn from it?

HISTORIAN

Is this helping at all? I don't know what painters look for.

PAINTER

You're being very helpful. I appreciate how honest you've been with me.

HISTORIAN

All right.

PAINTER

You should dubious.

HISTORIAN

I guess I don't see what you're getting out of this.

PAINTER

Quite honestly, it's part of my process. I don't think many people like saying this, but the majority of artists are scavengers. We take pieces from the world around us and mash them together. I don't want to paint just for myself, so I have to step outside my own wants and aesthetics, and think about what bothers other people. What haunts them, like the Ripper case haunts you.

HISTORIAN
I'm not a Ripperologist.
PAINTER
I know, but it's something you feel deeply about. And to be entirely cavalier about it, that's something I can use. That need to remember these women as they really were, when they've already been distorted into some strange myth. I don't think I'll sit down and paint Annie Chapman when we're done. I'm not that literal. But I'll be thinking about her as I work, about how deeply you feel for the truth of this case, and something will probably come of that.
HISTORIAN
I'm not sure I understand.
PAINTER
I know it's strange.
HISTORIAN
This work is strange.
PAINTER
You're quite right! But it is important, I think. Otherwise it might be lost.
HISTORIAN
I want someone to remember Annie Chapman as a person. Just one to remember her and not the Ripper.
The Painter smiles.
PAINTER
I promise at least one person will.
HISTORIAN
Thank you.
PAINTER
Shall we continue? There's still so much I want to ask you.
HISTORIAN
Yes. That would be all right. There's a lot to tell.
PAINTER
I'll do my best.
HISTORIAN
I know. Will you show me, when it's done?

  PAINTER

The painting?

                                        HISTORIAN

Yes.

                                        PAINTER

Of course.

                                        HISTORIAN

Then let's begin.

Blackout.

31

Pack Mentality

Yesterday he hurt you
broke teeth on a thoughtless word.
Tomorrow it might last.

You have always been careless with fear
though your hands are smaller
than even mine;

those small hands pried a bullet from a stranger's jaw,
once
You were not yet a doctor but
he lived.
Afterwards you touched my cheek, said
"What lonely teeth you have."

You married your husband on a holy day.
My lonely teeth stood witness, silent.
I pay penance now, for knowing.

You say it's nothing
because you have not yet bled
and certainly know better than me
the intricacies of bone.

And I grind my lonely teeth
seething and
silent.

An Atheist In Trump's Americana

Begin with,
> *What do you know? then,*
> *How do you know it?*

The poet accepts faith
the scholar takes citations
and the painter asks all questions
and sells too many answers

Continue:
> *What makes a good person? then,*
> *Are you among them?*

The skeptic says,
> *Are you moral because of God? then,*
> *Would you be moral without God?*

The historian remembers the crusades
those shining knights
> *(my darling, your holy men were rapists)*

The believer saves flags in the flood.
sang for God and Country
resilience through the muck.
> Asks, *How can you begrudge faith?*

> *Ah*, the poet says,
> *but faith is not always about God.*

What gives you comfort is no concern of mine.
> Here we say, *Do no harm*

and then we add,
> *But take no shit.*

A woman asked,
> *Have you heard the Word?*

My friend, I am a poet
I have heard too many.

She did not mind
a quota had been set
and if I would be so kind?

(I will not, indeed, be so kind)

Question:
> *What does God say to the holy liars?* then,
> *Can they be sainted if they only murder heathens?*

You should know, it was a believer who told me to
> *die, faggot,*
> *in your dirt*

alit in righteous fire

The woman said,
> *You would be sweeter with faith.*

The poet replied:
> *I have embraced my sour bones.*

Legendary Wolves:
In Memory Of Peter Stumpp's Daughter

Here's a riddle;
We don't believe in werewolves but history says
they still died
In Dole, then
Chalons and Germany,
1589
There were bystanders then, broken on the wheel
Peter's love and then his daughter too
but we are civilized here and
only believe in wolves when they live in zoos

Answer me this:
we don't believe in wolves but
who said it was time
to forget their daughters too?

Burn Notice

Doorknocker, boom. Did you hear?
Sorrow's got a girl living way out there.
Digging holes, killing rats. Running.

Nighttime, she goes rogue.
Writes letters to Rage.
Signs them *witch girl*,

never was a fool girl.

Did you hear?
She's gonna burn the world.
Did you hear?
She's gonna dance
and eat the ashes cold.

scene:
filmmaker seeks poet's advice on composition of sext to future wife

A friend brought her fried clams and
Mexican Cola, said this
was a metaphor for sex
Now help me write this text, faggot, I
am trying to seduce the girl
who sits by the door in Global Studies
and aren't you good with words?

She drank the coke with its cane sugar base
imported special
said, take her to the museum and mention
something about masterpieces, I
have never been in love with anyone
who loved me back
Why would you ask me anything
when you already know
the trick about clams?

The friend shrugged. Said,
I make movies, faggot
You write poems
Now help me sext this girl
before she becomes my muse

Various Thematic Punishments in the SAW Series

Distance from the world.	Dismemberment.
Bystander.	Bone snapped.
Stringent.	Drowned in gore.
Greed.	Pound of flesh.
Depression.	Bleeding.
Voyeur.	Starvation.
Grief.	Witness.
Addiction.	Relapse.
Bystander.	Burnt alive.
Mistake.	Repeated.
Survival.	Trauma.

How strange

                              to make it simple.

Halloween Prayer

come halloween and that house you'll hear
a townie girl died
right there by the door.

mythology says she wore red
grave says that's why she died
cracked her skull upon a no

our hallowed ghost
townie girl in your fine red dress,
in your death we pray:
keep us safe in the dark.

Artemisia Gentileschi,
Self Portrait As The Allegory of Painting (1639)

Dress in green, hair
half done
A painter's allegory
should always include some color

Remember me?
I was immortal once

In 1610, it's said
foreshadowing

A year later, truth from
true pain

I heard there ought to be some blood
on the history
otherwise it's not really
history

Remember me?
I am immortal once more
in all the wrong ways

A Babydyke's Primer to Slasher Films

The first and only thing to know;
all the women you meet are hungry
though only the bad ones go cannibal.
The survivors shed clothes, take knives
bleed to the bone
Turn, then
devour out of spite.

Do you love? You will die.
Don't love.

If you love regardless
Sever, child
and find yourself
Full of teeth.

Georgia O'Keeffe

Black hat style, all western
and a black dress in the
sun, for the bones

She made flowers strange, made skulls
pastel
Did you dream of ghosts, my dear?

In high school some girls dropped a book
in a barrel of ink
stained the flowers black
got detention
also: a legacy

Who else dreams of a ghost all in black,
wandering the desert strange?

Burial Ground

stand here a deer stand
dear *heart* we have
gone hunting
in the dark i heard
a boy died there, in the leaves
run dear, running
deer their
hooves chipped where the road ends
and the road ended where you stand
on the deer stand you will
leave flowers, dear heart,
won't you?

we won't be long.

mice inherit apocalypse

woke up sour on a thursday.
i dreamt a fishbowl universe where mice cohabitate with monkeys
except when the monkeys get hungry.
this is not a metaphor. call it nature.
darwin's gift house. or maybe
another weekday dream.

did you hear? the world's ending.
brimstone sold all their stock.
the monkeys crumble. the mice
cower, dreaming; maybe the cockroaches will
take them in.

Legendary Wolves: In Memory of Peter Stumpp's Daughter (Redux)

Characters

The Wolf   Both a beast and a young woman.

The Girl   Beele Stumpp, fifteen years old.

Scene I

The WOLF stands beneath a willow tree.
The stage is dark.

WOLF

This is factual: The werewolf trial of 1589 ended with one of the most brutal executions in German history. A farmer named either Peter Stumpp, Peter Stube, or Peter Stübbe was accused of killing fourteen children and two pregnant women while in the shape of a ravenous wolf. He was accused on account of his missing left hand, for the werewolf in question was missing a left forepaw. Peter was also a wealthy Protestant in a time and place where Protestants were suspect. Under torture, he confessed to practicing black magic, consorting with the Devil, and possessing a magic belt that allowed him to transform into a wolf. No such belt was ever found. He also confessed to having an incestuous relationship with his young daughter, whose name was either Beele or Sybil. She was likely fifteen years old. Both Peter, Beele, and Peter's lover, a woman whose name we do not know, were put to death on October 31st, 1589. Peter was broken on the wheel, his limbs shattered and his head removed, before he was then burned in a pyre. Beele and the woman Peter loved were flayed and strangled, their bodies burned. When it was done, a pole was erected carrying the torture wheel and a figure of a wolf as a warning against evil. Peter's head was placed on top.

No evidence has ever been found to support the guilt of Peter Stumpp, his daughter, or his unnamed lover.

The WOLF smiles.

All that is factual. And in some ways, this is true.

Begin.

Blackout.

Scene II

A GIRL lies under a willow tree, dead, a sheet over her face. A WOLF lies by her feet. The GIRL rises abruptly, kicking the sheet off.

GIRL

Wolf!

WOLF

Girl.

They circle each other.

GIRL

Am I—?

WOLF

Very. I dug you up. Don't think badly of me for that. I was very careful to put your bones back in place. You shouldn't feel any pain.

The girl touches her arms, her face, her hips.

GIRL

They said I did wicked things with a wolf. Not <u>you</u>, but a wolf. They said the wolf was my father.

WOLF

It was a cruel lie they told. Would my sorrow comfort you?

GIRL

No. Maybe. But I want somebody to be sorry. Have you ever been broken?

WOLF

Yes. But not like you.

GIRL

You have an answer for everything. It's so fucking <u>easy</u> for you, isn't it?

WOLF

I have seen this before.

GIRL

You witness

WOLF

I watch.

GIRL

Fuck you.

WOLF

If you like.

The Wolf lies down at her feet.

WOLF

I will not say you are stronger now.

GIRL

Then what am I?

WOLF

The aftermath.

GIRL

I suppose I should do something with that.

WOLF

By definition, martyrs never do anything with their fame.

GIRL

People worship martyrs like Christ.

WOLF

Blasphemy.

GIRL

They called me a whore. Broke my hips when they raped me. I cried for my father - who wouldn't? - and that, <u>that</u> was my confession, you see.

WOLF

I'm sorry.

GIRL

I don't <u>want</u> your sorrow.

WOLF

What then shall I lay at your feet?

GIRL

Nothing! Fuck you!

WOLF

I will bring you willow for your pain. Then, maybe, I will bring you teeth.

The Wolf turns abruptly.

WOLF

You were burned and scattered in the marsh. It took me a long time to stitch you back together, Peter's Daughter, and I'm afraid I could not find every piece. The dust of you will stick in the mud.

GIRL

And my aunt?

WOLF

The same. It's best you don't ask about your father.

GIRL

Why not?

WOLF

The memory is cruel.

GIRL

You don't get to decide that.

WOLF

I'm only saying.

GIRL

You owe me that much.

WOLF

I owe you?

The Wolf rises and moves to stand next to the Girl, guarding her.

WOLF

Maybe I do. Hmm. In time they will question his guilt. It won't matter, of course. But the world will wonder. They'll feel some sorrow for the legend.

GIRL

And me?

WOLF

They won't remember your name, Peter's Daughter. Your father killed children or your father was a sad man who did nothing at all. Whatever he did, Peter's Daughter bled on the pyre and lost her sorry head. It's assumed you suffered.

GIRL

It's assumed.

WOLF
Shall I give you teeth, my dear? I don't love you, but I'm here.

GIRL
What am I supposed to do with teeth?

WOLF
Hmm. Whatever a ghost does with fear.

GIRL
Oh my God, you're a fucking poet.

WOLF
Language.

GIRL
<u>Fuck</u> you.

WOLF
I never did. It seems a shame. We could have been wild together.

GIRL
I thought wolves only seduced virgins.

WOLF
Is that what you learned from Little Red?

GIRL
I don't know her.

WOLF
One day, everyone will. But I don't blame her. She was only a child.

GIRL
Oh.

WOLF
If I can be flippant? We love who we love. All this talk of virgins comes back to sacrifice. And we are beautiful - certainly, we are beautiful! - but we are wolves, my dear. Not gods.

GIRL
I thought it would matter to you.

WOLF
The sacrifice?

GIRL
Being a virgin.

WOLF
That is a human word.

GIRL
Oh.

They linger in silence.

GIRL
What would I do with teeth?

WOLF
Anything you please, except revenge. Dying is cruel that way.

GIRL
You're giving me useless teeth.

WOLF
Not useless, my love. I promise you'll be remembered.

GIRL
"My love."

WOLF
Perhaps. I would not be opposed to the idea.

GIRL
That doesn't change any of it. You're supposed to avenge me.

WOLF
I am not that kind of wolf. But...

A pause.

WOLF
I see no reason your memory should be <u>gentle</u>.

GIRL
Teeth, was it?

WOLF
And claws as well. Very sharp.

GIRL
How sharp?

WOLF
As sharp as your pain. Even God would flinch.

GIRL
I thought I was the blasphemer.

WOLF

I seduce, that much is true, but I never <u>lie</u>. These teeth are what you make of them: everything in the world except <u>gentle</u>.

The Girl examines her hands.

GIRL

I never had a lover, you know. I must not have been a very good whore.

The Wolf growls.

WOLF

That was not done out of love.

GIRL

Would you? "Do me" out of love?

WOLF

If you asked.

GIRL

You said I could do anything with teeth.

WOLF

Almost anything. You can haunt them, Peter's Daughter. Bleed their righteous dreams. You can watch from the tree, grind your sorrow down and rage with it. Or you can step away from it, my love, and I will teach you how to sing as wolves sing.

GIRL

I see.

WOLF

And what do you choose?

GIRL

I will have those teeth, I think.

WOLF

They will remember you. I promise.

The Wolf holds out a hand. The Girl takes it.

Blackout.

Ouroboros

I had a dream last night. My parents came home with a large glass terrarium. Inside there was a large green snake. It looked like a boa constrictor but in the dream it wasn't a boa constrictor. I couldn't be sure if it was venomous or not. The snake was going in this circle around the terrarium, counterclockwise, around and around and around again. Its spine was damaged. It could only move in circles. My mother said we would take it to the vet in the morning and I asked, isn't it in pain? There was a bump in the coils, you could see where something was broken inside. The snake went in its circles and my mother said, it might be. She couldn't be sure. But it was safe in the terrarium and nothing would try to eat it there. In the morning we'd take the big terrarium and carry it to the vet and he would fix the snake, with its broken back, and if there was pain - I knew there was pain - it wouldn't last. So I watched the snake going around and around the terrarium, broken spine bumping against the glass and I told it: *soon*.

Relic

Though the subgenre is commonly thought to have started with *The Blair Witch Project* in 1999, found footage horror planted its roots much earlier. The first example of the subgenre is Ruggero Deodato's *Cannibal Holocaust* (1980), followed closely by the *Guinea Pig* series in 1985. Many of these films have roots in both the American grindhouse and Italian giallo movements. In time, these artistic movements shifted into the modern age, advancing with technique and theory. They would eventually be dubbed extreme horror or "torture porn" by critics for their fascination with the human body and the many ways it might be broken. Both Ruggero Deodato and Hideshi Hino, one of the *Guinea Pig* directors, would be brought to court on murder charges, accused of making snuff films. They hadn't, though Deodato made the peculiar choice of insisting his actors take a paid vacation for several months after the release of *Cannibal Holocaust*. Historians are torn on how this impacted the film's actual ticket sales.

It's worth noting that *The Blair Witch Project* pulled the same stunt. The production team also released missing posters with the actors' faces and set up a tip-line for information pertaining to the case, borrowing tactics from a much more violent film. It's strange how found footage horror started off accused of snuff and then moved onto the art house. Regardless, this is where we come from.

Following the success of *The Blair Witch Project*, found footage horror saw a resurgence in American cinema. The rules of these films are simple and as follows:

> The audience accepts that the footage is shot by the characters themselves.
> The audience accepts that the footage is unedited.
> The audience knows the characters will not survive.

> Their last act—whether defiant, kind, or cowardly—will be to create a relic with their footage.
> The audience knows none of this is real but accepts it regardless for the sake of emotion following intimacy.

The creation of relics is not limited to film. Robert Landsburg, a photographer, was on Mount St. Helens when it erupted in May of 1980. Realizing he couldn't outrun the coming ash, his continued to shoot. His last act was to pack his camera away and lay on top of it, shielding the photographs with his body. It's commonly thought he suffocated.

I have heard this is a painful way to die. It would be seventeen days before Robert Landsburg's photographs or his body could be recovered.

This was an act of many things. I cannot name them. The photographs are considered of immense scientific value. They survive. In found footage, the audience accepts that the footage has survived. They do not assume it will be of value to anyone. The characters die. Their words endure. And do their words matter?

Someone certainly died for them.

Regardless. This is where we come from. This is how we go.

The audience assumes;
    we continue.

wrecker

riddle me: how might you hang the lantern
and so then see him done?
and by done we do mean dead, let's be clear

our history is thus: anyone can kill a ship, all hands drown
on the reef.
it only takes a lantern
a blue light on the horizon, then
rocks in the water, gold on the sand
it was a business once
people lived doing this.

i'll not be gentle now, i gave you something
blue once, a sunday sight
and darling, my darling
it should have been a knife.

i am sorry it was not a knife

answer me, she said
do you hate men?

in truth, i said,
i do not hate my father.

but the husband, in contrast,
is easy.

solve me, friend.
i cannot know your life.
i would have downed his ship
(metaphorically) all the way
but we are honest now;
know this is not a kindness

riddle me: what must I do with this lantern for you?
this piece of something borrowed
and oh so
      (blue)

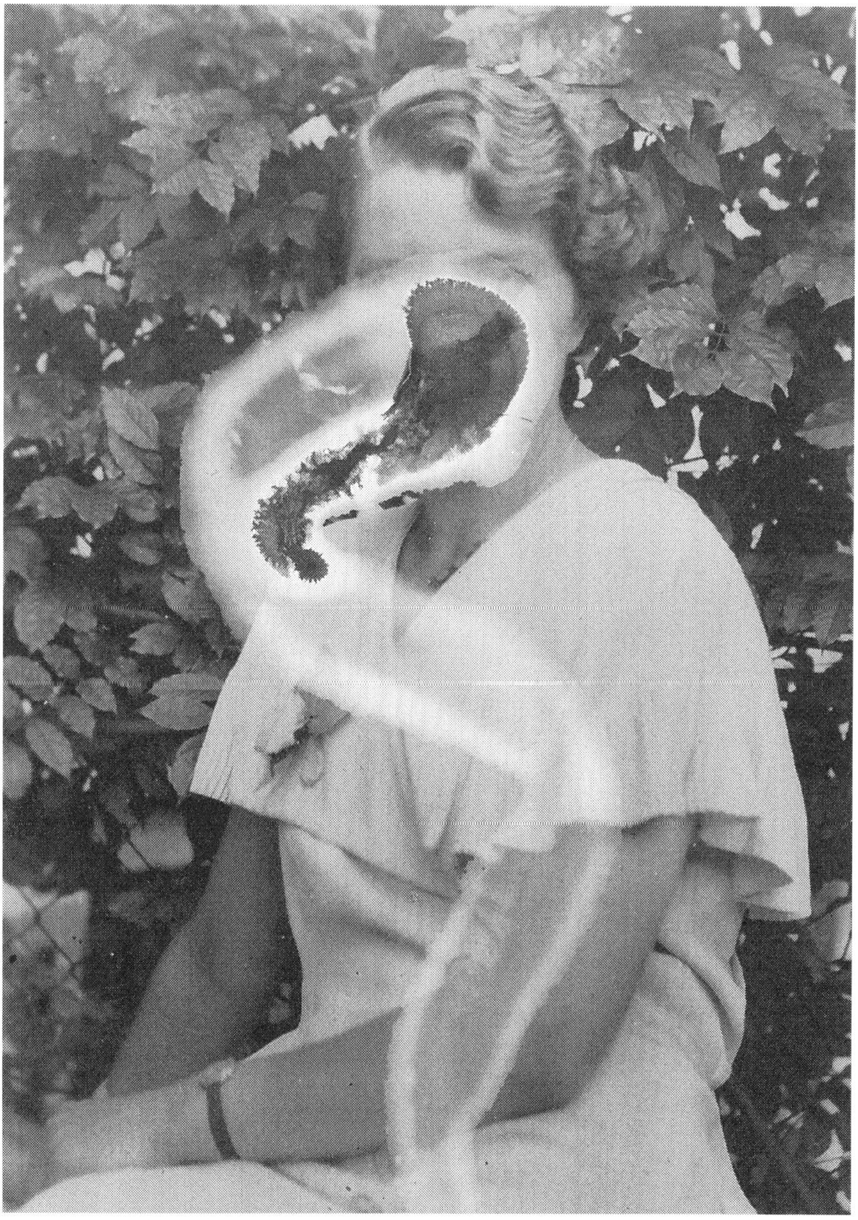

About the Author

Emma Johnson-Rivard is a Masters student at Hamline University. She currently lives in Minnesota with her dogs and far too many books. Her work has appeared in Mistake House, the Nixes Mate Review, and Moon City Review.

Made in the USA
Middletown, DE
01 July 2019